PILGRIM · GUIDE

✠

TINTERN

Other titles in the Pilgrim Guide series

PILGRIM · GUIDE

TINTERN

Esther de Waal

Illustrated by
Chris Jarvis

CANTERBURY
PRESS
Norwich

Text © Esther de Waal 1999
Illustrations © Chris Jarvis 1999

First published in 1999 by The Canterbury Press Norwich
(a publishing imprint of Hymns Ancient & Modern Limited
a registered charity)
St Mary's Works, St Mary's Plain
Norwich, Norfolk NR3 3BH

British Library Cataloguing in Publication Data

A catalogue record for this book is available
from the British Library

ISBN 1-85311-312-3

Typeset by Rowland Phototypesetting Ltd,
Bury St Edmunds, Suffolk
Printed and bound in Great Britain by
Redwood Books, Trowbridge, Wilts

Contents

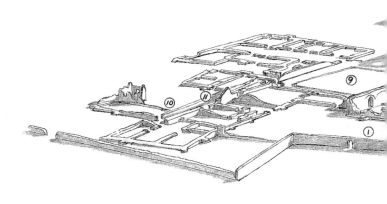

Before Starting – A Short Time of Recollection

Each one of us comes to this place with open hands,
                                    open eyes,
                                    open heart,
ready and open to receive whatever there may be waiting for us in these stones, any message or insight that they may carry.

This abbey was built by men of the Christian faith in a place of the greatest beauty. They were aware of the presence of God in their lives in a way that does not come so easily and naturally for many of us today.

I am after all not even sure who I am, let alone who God might be. But I want to walk quietly, my feet touching the earth gently, my hands ready to feel the texture of stones, moss, wood; my eyes attentive to changing light and shape; above all, my heart listening – for what? I do not yet know.

Roof boss

I The Situation

Every visitor to Tintern is arrested by their first sight of this ruined abbey, romantically set in a valley of hanging woods beside the magnificent sweep of the river Wye. It captures the imagination today as it has always done, particularly for the 18th-century Romantic poets and artists who enthused about it so ecstatically.

This splendid geographical site gives us the best starting point if we want to understand the vision of those founding monks who arrived here in the 12th century. It would then have been a remote, wild part of the countryside, still largely uncolonized, which was exactly what they were looking for. When Tintern was founded as a Cistercian abbey on 9 May 1131, it was only the second house in the whole country and the first in Wales, to belong to the Cistercian order. This was the latest monastic reforming movement whose mother house, Cîteaux, had only been established in France a little over thirty years earlier, in March 1098.

The Cistercians were known as White Monks because of their white habits of undyed wool which were a symbol of their determination to return to a pristine and more pure observance of the Rule of St Benedict as it had been first written in the 6th century, cutting loose from all the accretions and additions that it had since acquired. The monastic life envisioned by St Benedict was of a community of men or women, earning their living by manual labour, finding time for daily study, but essentially putting the work of God, *opus Dei* or prayer, at the heart of their lives. This was a life of balance of body, mind and spirit, in working with the hands, in using the mind, but above all in the work of praying which took them seven times a day into the church, for the singing of the psalms and the listening to the reading of scripture that took priority as the foundation of everything else that they did. It was a holistic way of life, for they did not make the separation (so common in much later religion) of the material and the spiritual. The pattern of their life was based on showing respect and reverence for the earth itself, for the changing seasons and the times of day and night, for their tools and the things that they handled, and not least for the human body itself. They recognized the importance of rhythm and of good order in daily life, and of living together in a way that expressed loving relationships between one another.

But, as so often in the history of the Church, as time goes on an institution becomes attractive, popular and too comfortable. The Benedictines by the 11th century had become extremely wealthy and successful, acquiring property which they farmed extremely efficiently; they had amassed large libraries, they ran schools, and as a result they found themselves becoming rather too involved with the secular society around them, and not least beholden to local rich patrons. It was to escape from this, and to return to a life of greater austerity and simplicity, that a small group of Benedictine monks in Burgundy left their monastery and set out for 'the desert' – a symbol of the return to purity of heart. In this case, the place itself was also an actual wilderness, as they tell us in their original account: 'a wilderness where men rarely penetrated and none but wild things lived'. This they felt would suit their purpose well, for they hoped that in this unattractive and desolate part of the country, far from the haunts of other people, they might be able to regain something of what that first monastic impulse had been.

Their success was astounding. These men in their white habits descended upon Europe like flocks of white birds, as a monk of the Yorkshire Cistercian abbey of Rievaulx so charmingly put it. Soon their first foundation at Citeaux had daughter houses and more and more new foundations followed quickly. Undoubtedly one of the reasons for their success was the extent to which they were so much in tune with their age. The 12th century was a time of vitality and energy in many directions, a time of growth and exploration and of experimentation in architecture. Above all it was a time of intellectual excitement which came with the growth of the universities, the wandering scholars, and the new learning which thrived as translations of hitherto unknown works of

The approach

Plato and Aristotle brought fresh tools for intellectual debate. The population explosion of these years meant not only urban development and better communications but the search for new land, frequently marginal or waste land, which could be reclaimed and cultivated.

The Cistercians responded to both the intellectual and the economic thrusts. Influenced by the intellectual revival they studied ancient texts as fresh and living books, returning to the well-springs of the Rule of St Benedict with new questions and demands which opened it up afresh. But as well as the highly educated choir monks (and soon the Order was to produce men of skilled and sophisticated literary abilities), the Cistercians also welcomed into the Order lay brothers – a complete innovation. These were humble men, of peasant stock, illiterate and uneducated, who had not hitherto been included in a monastic life which had expected literacy and a knowledge of Latin. These men now brought to the community the skill of their hands, their experience in farming and husbandry, and their knowledge of marketing or of engineering and building. But all, choir monks and lay brothers alike, shared in a common vocation: to live the life of the gospel as it was set out in the Rule of St Benedict in all its simplicity and fullness.

Tintern was founded from l'Aumone, in northern France, an abbey which was itself a daughter house of Citeaux, thus making Tintern the granddaughter, as it were, of the mother house of the whole Order. A local lord, Walter Fitz Richard of Clare, the Anglo-Norman lord of Chepstow, invited an abbot and twelve monks (the usual pattern, following that of Christ and the twelve disciples), together with some lay brothers, and Tintern was founded on 9 May 1131. Eight years later in 1139, after this small beginning, they had become sufficiently established to found their own daughter house, in Kingswood in Gloucestershire, for by this date the number of choir monks had grown to sixty in addition to a large number of lay brothers. These latter were undoubtedly extremely significant in accounting for Tintern's success since they had been granted a considerable amount of land on both sides of the Wye, mostly marginal land on which they had to clear and fell timber, or undertake necessary draining and ditching in the low-lying marshy areas, in order to establish viable farming, above all the pastures for their large flocks of sheep. They had also soon established mills for grinding corn and forges for making iron. Their more distant lands were centred on small 'granges' (before long there were ten of them) where a handful of lay brothers lived very simply with one or two essential buildings, such as a barn or a sheep cote, possibly a stable for a horse, or a water-mill, and of course an oratory.

By the end of the 13th century they were farming over three thousand acres and by the end of the Middle Ages the desert had blossomed and the Wye valley would have looked very different indeed from what the founding monks had first seen in 1131. The abbey precinct itself had grown to 27 acres, with a series of enclosed courts and walled enclosures, surrounded by an outer wall which rose to ten feet. This was broken by two outer gateways, the second along the water frontage leading to a river slipway with a ferry crossing. The outer court held stables, barns, granaries, and houses for cattle and oxen. The nearby Angidy valley had meanwhile become a hive of activity with a grinding mill, a fulling mill, fishing weirs, beehives and a tannery.

A century later much of the original spiritual drive had disappeared, and by the 1530s, on the eve of the Dissolution of the monasteries by Henry VIII, numbers had shrunk. On 3 September 1536 the last abbot, Richard Wyche, was given a pension, and the twelve remaining choir monks and the thirty-five monastic servants likewise received sums of money. The Abbey's possessions were dispersed and the buildings themselves were granted to Henry Somerset, Earl of Worcester. He had no reason to live there himself, already owning castles at both Chepstow and Raglan, and so instead he let out tenements and parcels of land to tenants who must have made themselves makeshift homes under the Gothic arches. In the 1560s a new industrial era began at Tintern with the production of iron wire using water power, but that is not part of the story of the Cistercian abbey itself.

The General Approach

Entering Tintern through the modern official entrance is a bewildering introduction to any understanding of the abbey, for the first impression is that of being confronted by a mass of ruins, sprawling and opening up in all directions. It is a good moment to stop and try to find the key to unlock the meaning of what might otherwise seem little better than the remains of a succession of apparently random buildings. That key of course lies in the vision and intentions of the monks who built this place, which we considered in the introduction. For these are essentially functional buildings designed to serve a particular way of life, buildings whose purpose will unfold as we walk around them.

The fact that the abbey was built so beautifully, and with such care that much still remains today, tells us immediately something important. 'Handle all things and all people with reverence and respect' might be a good way of summarizing the monastic attitude towards both things and people. The Cistercians were men who respected matter and material things, they handled time with care, attentive to the coming of day and night, the rhythm of dark and light, the pattern of the changing seasons. They felt close to the earth, they were grounded in one place by their vow of stability (to remain in one place for life) so they were quite naturally united to their immediate environment, both to the buildings and the landscape.

Two of the Cistercian vows are those of stability and *conversatio morum*. They immediately present us with a paradox since stability, coming from the word *stare*, means to stand, to remain, not only geographically but also interiorly, firm and still; while *conversatio* means conversion, transformation, being open to change, always moving on and being open to what is new. This holding together of standing still but also moving forward to new locations and the insights which they bring gives us a useful guideline for our journey around Tintern, making it something of a pilgrimage, not only into a building but into a way of life and a vision of God.

As we let ourselves be drawn by these doors and arches which now open up before us it becomes important that we also take time. The monastic tradition in whatever culture, whether Buddhist or Christian, knows about mindfulness, attentiveness, being present, being alive to the world around and seeing the visible as a reflection of the invisible.

Thomas Merton was a 20th-century monk who lived the Cistercian life in the abbey of Gethsemani in Kentucky, and there learnt much about seeing the world around him in stillness, not rushing, not wanting to possess, but instead developing the quiet eye and quiet mind.

I need to slow down as I walk around these ruins. Time is not important. 'We don't have to rush after it,' Merton tells us. 'Above all, don't be worried about the pace.' If I want to see into the heart of this place, and let it reveal its essence to me, I must take time, because 'if I give it time it will make itself known to me'.

A tomb in the Abbey Church

The Cloisters

We are now standing in what was the hub of the community's life. Originally covered passageways for reading and meditation would have run along each side, offering the monks some protection from the elements as they sat here doing their prayer-filled, reflective study, *lectio divina*. The first word of the Rule of St Benedict which the monks followed is *Listen*, and the monk started each day with the verse from Psalm 95, 'Today if you will hear my voice harden not your heart.' Hearing the words of scripture, reading and pondering them in the heart, allowed them then to listen and to respond to God in a continuous dialogue. The monastic vow of obedience comes from the word *ob audiens*, meaning to listen intently, so that obedience is simply listening to the voice of God, hearing it and responding.

The open space which we see here gives us an illuminating image of monastic life. What other set of buildings puts emptiness at its heart? It speaks of the emptiness which each monk tried to carry within himself, an open, uncluttered space in his own heart so that he might listen to the Word of God. The monastic garden within the cloisters carries the image further, a metaphor for the cultivation needed throughout all the changing seasons, of the year and of life, if that garden were to grow and flourish and bear fruit.

From this central point there now opens up the

whole range of buildings serving the needs of daily life. The Rule of St Benedict knows that each person is made up of body, mind and spirit, and that due attention should be paid to each of these elements as God-given. So in one corner we can see the dormitory in which the monks slept in a great open hall-like space above the day room where they worked. Moving further west we find the refectory and next to it the kitchen. St Benedict was very clear how important it was to take the needs of the body seriously and he insisted on enough sleep (eight hours a night) and good simple vegetarian food, carefully prepared and served with a choice of dishes or allowances for any who needed them. In the chapter room, on the east side, the community would meet each morning to read a chapter of the Rule before they settled down together to deal with the administrative business about the maintenance of the property, farming, finances, and other decisions about their common life, including the correction of faults.

Walking round the cloisters we can see them as a sort of link-line uniting the succession of buildings that served the monks' daily needs: sleep, food, work, study, business – but above all prayer. For seven times a day they would leave everything else and, passing through the cloisters, go into the church to say the seven daily offices that gave their life its distinctive framework. It is as though the church anchors all the other daily activities, for there is a continual movement between praying and working.

Here, in another spatial image, is the interplay between stable places and the pathways that link them, bringing this gentle rhythm and interplay of time and space from which flowed the Cistercian life of unity and cohesion.

I feel that I live much of my life under pressure. I seem to have lost any sense of rhythms and balance. What simple wisdom the Cistercians have in recognizing the importance of paying attention to body, mind and spirit, seeing each of these three elements as God-given and to be taken seriously. Can I learn from them?

What would it mean in my own life if I were to try to bring something of this same pattern into my day – time for working with my hands, for using my mind, for setting aside for prayer?

II The Church

The East End

In the later 13th and early 14th centuries thirty years were spent in building a brand new church to take the place of a modest Romanesque church whose remains can still be traced on the ground to the north of the present church. The master mason was faced with a difficult task since he had to build this new church in a way that would allow the monks to continue to worship in the existing church for as long as possible. When the eastern part of the new church was sufficiently advanced the monks moved into the newly finished choir and presbytery, celebrating their first mass at the high altar on 3 October 1288. After this the building was continued westwards, which involved pulling down the old church and reusing the stone for the new work.

In our own journey it seems a good idea to start with the east end and to go, as the masons would have done, towards the west end. Our starting point, the most easterly part of the church, is rather confusingly known as the presbytery. It stretched the length of three bays from the east window to the crossing, and its main focal point was the high altar itself above which towers the great east window.

The East Window

This is one of the glories of Tintern, a triumph of architectural design with its vast eight-light window, the head surmounted by three roundels or oculi (*oculus* is the Latin word for eye). The whole impulse of the monk's life was to be awake, alive, attentive. St Benedict was looking for men whose lives were open, not closed up, and that meant being open not only to the scriptures but also to nature. It was an old monastic saying that God was to be found both in the Word and in nature, and a familiar saying attributed to St Bernard, one of the greatest of all the early Cistercians, was 'You will find among the woods something you never found in books.' The Romantics liked to come here at night in order to view the full moon, particularly the harvest moon, through that central roundel. They were in fact, however distantly, doing just as the monks had done, being in tune with time and with creation. The Cistercians worshipped a God who was part of the natural order of creation, and their lives were naturally shaped and integrated into that order. These three roundels or eyes at the east end of their church remind us of how the monks here lived, open to the landscape around them, to the changing seasons, to the coming of light and the falling of darkness.

Standing here and looking to the left, to the north transept, we can see the doorway high in the wall of the night stairs that led from the dormitory down

The East Window

into the church. Each day at about 2 a.m. the monks came down those stairs to sing the first office of the day, Vigils, the name itself speaking of being vigilant, alert, awake. Each day therefore began in the dark, and that movement from darkness (not only of night and sleep but also of being unheeding and unaware) to light and new life tells us much about the monks' lives as well as about their prayers.

Under the Crossing

The open space that we now see would have been very different indeed in the Middle Ages, for originally solid stone screen walls between two rows or arcade piers ran the whole length of the building and divided the centre from the aisles on either side. In addition to this the central space itself was further divided by an elaborate screen or pulpitum, carrying highly decorative carving, which stood 18 feet high, and was added to the nave around 1320.

There were thus within the church itself several distinct areas used for definite and different functions. The central portion, both literally and also symbolically, was the choir which was the area which occupied the space between the site of the original pulpitum and the east end. It is best to think of it as a church set within a church, surrounded as it would have been by those screen walls. The monks could enter through a door in the middle of the

Night Stairs

19

pulpitum or else through a gap in the northern screen and then make their way to their heavy oak choir stalls. There they would sit in order and rank according to the date when they joined the community and seven times each day say the daily offices, beginning with Vigils before dawn and ending with Compline, before they went to bed, to make the day complete.

The Western Portion

Moving westwards, between the fourth and fifth bays came the retrochoir, in which the aged and infirm monks were allowed to sit during the offices. It occupied the space of one bay between the pulpitum, which marked the end of the choir and presbytery, and what marked the east end of the lay brothers' church, the rood screen – rood being the old word for cross since it carried an image of Christ on the cross, which has however now disappeared.

Probably the most significant division in the church was this, between the lay brothers and the rest of the community. The lay brothers used the back of the church, entering through a doorway set in the far north-west corner and then through a door in a break in the first bay of the screen. They were not expected to say the seven full offices. Theirs was a more simplified life of prayer, as befitted men who had such a heavy manual workload: they would recite the Lord's Prayer and the Agnus Dei.

The Crossing in the Abbey Church

The rough and natural colour of the stones today gives a misleading impression, for they would have been originally plastered with white lime with lines picked out in red, depicting imitation stonework (which you can see at Abbey Dore, another Cistercian abbey, in the Golden Valley not far from here). Thus the walls would have been brightly coloured, as would much of the floor, covered with a richly decorated pavement of glazed tiles. The arches of the vaulted roof met in the key stones with bosses, some of which can be seen lying on the ground, a number with naturalistic leaf-like designs, and they also would have been painted. This immediately dispels what is one of the most widely held misconceptions about Cistercian life – and monastic life in general – that it is gloomy, life-denying. Light, both actually and symbolically, was vital in Cistercian life, and we should picture the way in which the church would have made a vivid statement about the importance of living light and colour, celebration, praise.

Here I am carried into celebration and praise – in the words of one of the greatest traditional hymns of the church, a life-giving hymn, Te Deum Laudamus:

> We praise you, O God,
> we acclaim you as the Lord.
>
>> Everlasting Father
>> all the world bows down before you.
>
> All the angels sing your praise,
> the hosts of heaven and all the angelic powers,
>
>> all the cherubim and seraphim
>> call out to you in unending song:
>
>> Holy, Holy, Holy,
>> is the Lord God of hosts!
>
> The heavens and the earth are filled
> with your majesty and glory.

As I stand facing East I am thinking of the rising of the sun, the daily mystery of the movement from dark to light. These are images that take me beyond words. There are many thoughts crowding in on me at this point: a longing for darkness, pain, suffering and death to give way to res-urrection and new life – in so many areas of my life as well as of the wider world. A prayer need not be expressed in words – it is simply the offering up of something that goes beyond words.

The West Front

This must be one of the most glorious features not only of Tintern but of any great Gothic church anywhere. It is a work of outstanding beauty, and when it was completed around the year 1300 was one of the great architectural achievements of its day. At the bottom is the wide central doorway, which would have been used for processions. The panels on either side have very pretty decorative carving and above them hangs an almond-shaped niche, in which there would have been a carving of the Blessed Virgin Mary. Above the door rises a vast window with seven lights drawing the eye upwards to those three great roundels which complete the design. Finally there comes that huge window which would have filled the top of the nave with light. The whole composition has about it a sense of harmonious and ordered design – which should not surprise us since the Cistercians knew about order: in the regularity and rhythm of daily life, in the relationships which they cultivated in the community, and not least in the hierarchy which tied all the houses of the Order into one neat chain. I do not think it fanciful to see this great west front as a statement in stone of these values – and not least of the discipline and restraint which is an essential element in any true unity and harmony.

But order is not the same thing as safe or dull uniformity. There is vitality here, a sense of upward

Doorway of the West Front

thrusting movement, of soaring shapes full of energy. And there is delicacy too, in the detailed decoration of the gently flowing movement of the arches. At the centre of the doorway itself is that almond-shaped niche in which the monks placed a statue of St Mary. Every Cistercian church is dedicated to her: she held a central place in their affection. They wrote hymns to her and ended every day by singing the *Salve Regina* in her honour; they kept her festivals, they modelled themselves on what the gospel told them of her love and humble gentleness. Towards the end of the Middle Ages it seems likely that a pilgrimage chapel was built in front of the church – a few column bases can be seen in the ground in front as evidence of an elaborate 15th-century porch which was added, with probably above it the chapel containing a statue of our Lady.

Mary, the Mother of God, played an important part in the life of the Cistercians. 'Think of how much confidence we can have in her,' said Aelred, abbot of Rievaulx, for to them she was not some remote Queen of Heaven but a woman who was an example to inspire and support, and to whom it was entirely natural to pray:

Let us confidently beseech her and place our trust
    in her . . .
Let her be our common joy,
    our common glory,
    our common hope,
    our common consolation . . .
If we are sad, let us fly to her so that she may
    gladden us,
If we are disheartened, let us fly to her so that she
    may make us cheerful,
If we are in despair, let us fly to her so that she
    may raise us up,
If we are troubled, let us fly to her so that she may
    console us.
Let her be our guardian in this life and our
    protection at death.

III The West Range

Leaving the west window we return to the cloisters by way of a later 13th-century porch which has a stone bench on its south side and a stone vault added in the 15th century. This leads into the outer parlour, where visitors would have been received. No monastery was without its guests, pilgrims, wayfarers, those in need. One of the most famous aphorisms of the Rule was St Benedict's saying that everyone who came was to be received as Christ himself.

In the corner the space allocated to the lay brothers shows us how in practice the Cistercians included in their life men who had hitherto been given no place in the monastic life. The *conversi* or lay brothers were men drawn from the ranks of the local peasantry, skilled in farming, building, forestry or trade, but lacking any formal education. They wore a simple belted robe and unlike the cleanshaven monks were bearded. The pattern of their daily life was naturally rather different, the time they spent in church much shorter, with simpler prayers, and the working hours longer. But the constitutions decreed that they would be treated 'in life and in death as themselves', i.e. as the choir monks, and on all the major festivals the whole community would gather together, making a statement about the common vision underlying their differing vocations.

It is difficult to realize from the little that is left above ground just how large these buildings would have been: but the lay brothers would have had a refectory on the ground floor, next to the kitchen, and above it their dormitory and a small court which served as their cloister. Many of course would not be living here permanently but were scattered in the number of granges, which were rather like small out-lying rural homestead settlements, each with a small church, a barn, and a few simple buildings where a handful of these lay brothers would work and pray.

As I imagine the lay brothers, simply the ordinary local peasants, working the land, keeping sheep, milling, engaged in all the many aspects of husbandry, I think of how close the Cistercians always were to the earth, how they saw it as a gift of God to be handled with reverence and respect. In the face of the greed, exploitation and destruction of the earth's resources today, I want here to recall their appreciation of the earth as a gift of God, and the sense of wonder that that evokes. It seems suitable here to use something taken from the Celtic tradition, a 9th-century Welsh poem of praise to the Creator:

Almighty Creator, it is you who have made
the land and the sea . . .

The world cannot comprehend in song bright and
    melodious,

even though the grass and trees should sing,
all your wonders, O true Lord!

The Father created the world by a miracle;
it is difficult to express its measure,
letters cannot contain it, letters cannot
    comprehend it.

He who made the wonder of the world
will save us, has saved us.
It is not too great a toil to praise the Trinity.

The Chapter House

Crossing the cloisters diagonally we come to the large and splendid chapter house. Sit on the stone bench and imagine what it would have been like to be a member of the monastic community, coming here each day and seeing ranged round the wall all those other members with whom you would be living, working, eating, sleeping and praying for twenty, thirty, forty years. This was a household, an extended family, bound together in love, and an essential part of the learning and growing into that relationship of love was to listen daily to a chapter of the Rule of St Benedict (hence the name 'chapter house') which established the guidelines making such a shared life possible. There are shared decisions to be made about the common life, the maintenance of property, the

The Chapter House

balancing of the budget, and any matters concerning business and administration as well as personal misdoings and faults.

What we see today is a 13th-century rebuilding in a handsome fashion to reflect the importance that the chapter house played in the daily life of the monks. The entrance from the cloisters is striking, with its three highly decorated archways. Inside the roof was given rib vaulting supported on eight slender, elegant columns which divided the room into three bays across its width and five bays along its length. The room was lit by a series of tall windows set in the eastern wall. The floor would have been covered with a decorative tile pavement and some can still be seen in the borders. And here, under the floor, it was the Cistercian custom to bury their abbot. The abbot was the *abba* or father of this family, and what could be more suitable than for him to be laid to rest in a place which was the primary gathering place for the community?

✠

As they lived at close quarters with those whom they never would have chosen, monastic life in community taught the Cistercians much about relationships, about loving one another, about the role that the love of God plays in human relationships. One of the greatest of the 12-century Cistercians in this country was Aelred, abbot of Rievaulx in Yorkshire. This is what he wrote out of his experience, and to help the brothers in his care:

God himself is at work
pouring out between himself and the creatures he
    has raised up,
between the various hierarchies of his creation,
and between each and every one of his elect,
such reciprocal friendship and charity
that each loves the other as himself.
Each, in consequence, rejoices in his neighbour's
    happiness as his own,
so that the bliss of each is shared by all.

The Infirmary

It is very restful to sit on the bench here in front of the
infirmary cloister, in this the most secluded part of
the monastery, with the hills opening up behind, and
to think of the importance given to this part of the
monastic complex. Here the old and decrepit, those
suffering from any illness or disease and those
temporarily incapacitated by blood-letting, would be
received and cared for. Again the Rule was very clear
about the way in which the sick and the old were to
be looked after – for St Benedict addressed human
weakness and frailty and recognized it as part of the
human condition, not anything to be denied or
sidelined. He always showed special concern for
those needing help and support, and insisted on
courtesy and respect for the aged. It is not surprising
therefore to find how impressive the infirmary hall

The Infirmary

was, probably the most attractive building on the whole monastic complex after the church. It was built in the middle of the 13th century with a great central nave, over 100 feet long, and with wide aisles on either side. These housed the beds, and were divided by wooden partitions or hangings to give some measure of privacy.

Somewhere near there would have been a garden with the herbs and medicinal plants used for healing, about which the monks showed such skill and knowledge.

✠

Here is a place in which I want to stop and spend a few moments thinking about my own vulnerability and frailty, the woundedness and weakness which so often I would prefer to deny or to hide. I ask for healing in the words of a prayer which, as so often with these 12th-century Cistercians, comes close to poetry. John of Forde was the abbot of an abbey on the Dorset/Devon border, also in the west country. As he speaks of the healing tree of the cross he takes the apple tree that was always thought of as being particularly rich and abundant, and of course especially so in this part of the country. As we place ourselves in its warm shadow the dead wood becomes living wood which brings healing.

After we had lain so long in the shadow of death
God's Son came, pitying those who lay in
    darkness.
He made us lie down
under the shadow of another apple tree,
and by that shadow
as much as by its fruits
he raised us to life again.
He came that we may have life
and have it more abundantly.

The Abbot's Quarters

Finally in the furthest corner we have a group of
buildings associated with the abbot and the more
public role that he played in the separate accommo-
dation that was made available to him from the 13th
century on. His growing status is reflected in the 14th-
century developments when he had many guests
to entertain in style and comfort. Doors, mouldings
and buttresses all speak of a lavish style, though little
is left now and we can only guess at the extent of
the glory.

Here we have a comment on the growing style and
wealth of the monastery, a reflection of its increasing
wealth and economic prosperity.

The Abbot's Hall, with Chapel in the background

Drains

The romantic setting and the poetry of the Romantic poets about Tintern might have predisposed us to imagine the monastic life as a life of 'Gothic mystery'. Nothing could be further from the truth. These were down-to-earth men, competent and pragmatic. They ran a functional community effectively, using all their skill and expertise with sound efficiency. So it is fitting that in this final stage of our pilgrimage we should be paying homage to their drains.

The way in which they organized the drainage system of their abbeys is one of the best examples of their practical engineering skills. There was a saying 'Bernard in the valley, Benedict on the hill' which reminds us just how often the Cistercians were to be found near water, in valleys. As a result they were particularly skilled in the hydraulic systems which we can still see today. You have only to look at the existing arches to see what care they used in the construction. The latrine block lay near the day room, a two-storey building so that the dormitory led on to a row of privies on the first floor directly above the drainage sewer below. The main drain was flushed out by water possibly drawn from a spring called Coldwell above the abbey.

One of the advantages of belonging to an international order was that all its abbeys, however remote, were kept closely in touch with one another and with the centre, through an excellent communications system, not unlike multi-nationals today. This meant that knowledge of new techniques and the latest technological advances could be quickly diffused and shared.

Drains are not generally seen – they are hidden, underground. Yet just to stay here for a moment looking at these stones, noticing the care with which they were laid, the attention to the details of engineering and efficiency, is